Recipes from Community

By Community of Little Ducks Annerley
in collaboration with JBus
Illustrated by Nerida Groom

We respect and honour Aboriginal and Torres Strait Islander Elders past, present and future. We acknowledge the stories, traditions and living cultures of Aboriginal and Torres Strait Islander peoples on this land and commit to building a brighter future together.

Library For All Ltd.

Apple and Cinnamon Damper

Ingredients:

- 3 cups of self-raising flour
- ½ teaspoon of salt
- 1 teaspoon of white sugar
- 75g of chilled butter, cubed
- ¼ cup of brown sugar, firmly packed
- 1½ teaspoons of cinnamon
- 2 Gala or Pink Lady apples, grated
- 1 egg white, beaten
- ½ cup of milk
- ½ cup of cold water

4

Method:

1. Preheat the oven to 180° Celsius.
2. Grease a baking tray and line it with baking paper.
3. Mix the flour, salt, sugars and cinnamon in a bowl. After washing your hands, use your fingertips to rub the butter cube into the flour mixture until the mixture looks like breadcrumbs.
4. Add the grated apple and mix well. You can use your hands for this too, but make sure they're clean!
5. Add the milk and water to the flour and apple mixture. Mix until it forms a sticky dough.

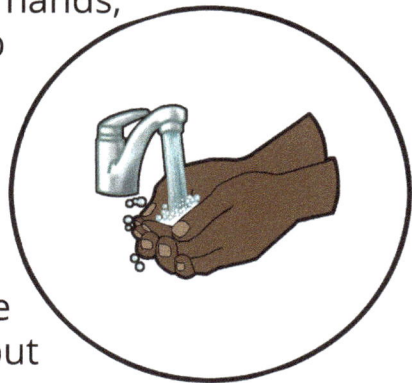

6. Put the dough on a lightly floured surface, then gently knead it with your clean hands until it's smooth (about four times).
7. Shape the dough into a circle, about 15–20 centimetres across.
8. Place the dough on the baking tray and put it in the oven.

9. Bake for 1 hour and 10 minutes. When you take it out of the oven, tap the bread. If it sounds hollow, it's ready.
10. Let the bread stand on the tray for 5 minutes, and then place it on a wire rack to cool.
11. Slice and serve with butter, banana, and maple syrup!

Banana and Wattle Seed Cake

Ingredients:

- 100g of low-fat margarine or butter
- ½ cup of white sugar
- 2 eggs
- 2 cups of self-raising flour, sifted
- 1 tablespoon of wattle seeds
- ½ cup of low-fat milk
- 2 ripe bananas, mashed

Method:

1. Preheat the oven to 180° Celsius.
2. Coat a loaf tin with cooking spray.
3. Beat the margarine and sugar together until they look creamy.
4. Add the eggs, and then beat these ingredients together until smooth.

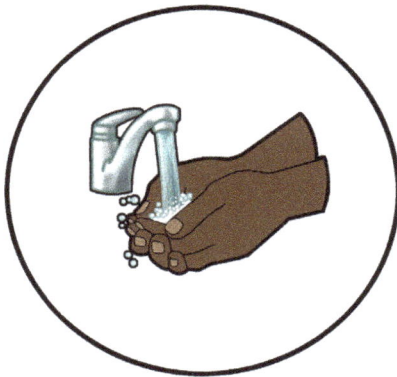

5. Add the mashed banana and wattle seeds and mix, before folding in the milk and flour.

6. Spoon the mixture into the prepared tin and bake in the oven for 30 minutes, or until golden.

Lemon Myrtle Biscuits

Ingredients:

- 250g of sugar
- 250g of butter
- 500g of self-raising flour
- 4 eggs OR 4 tablespoons of egg replacer
- 25g of ground lemon myrtle

Method:

1. Preheat the oven to 180° Celsius.
2. Prepare a baking tray with baking paper laid on it.
3. Beat the butter and sugar together until they look creamy.
4. Add the eggs (or the replacer) into the mix one at a time.

5. After washing your hands, use your fingers to pick up small handfuls of the mixture, rolling it into small balls.

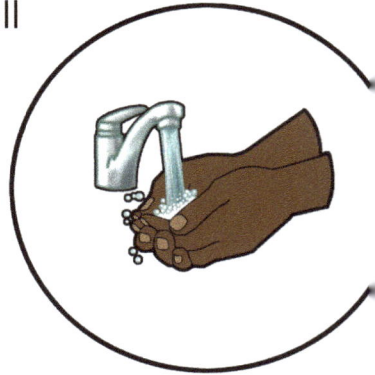

6. Put the balls on the baking tray. Sprinkle some flour on a fork and use it to press the batter down on the tray.
7. Bake for 12–15 minutes.

You can use these questions to talk about this book with your family, friends and teachers.

What did you learn from this book?

Describe this book in one word. Funny? Scary? Colourful? Interesting?

How did this book make you feel when you finished reading it?

What was your favourite part of this book?

About the contributors

These stories were generously shared by the community at Little Ducks Childcare Annerley, Queensland, after they enjoyed an Our Yarning story sharing session.

JBus is a Gubbi Gubbi woman from Queensland and lives in Brisbane. She enjoys being at the beach with her family, creating art and singing.

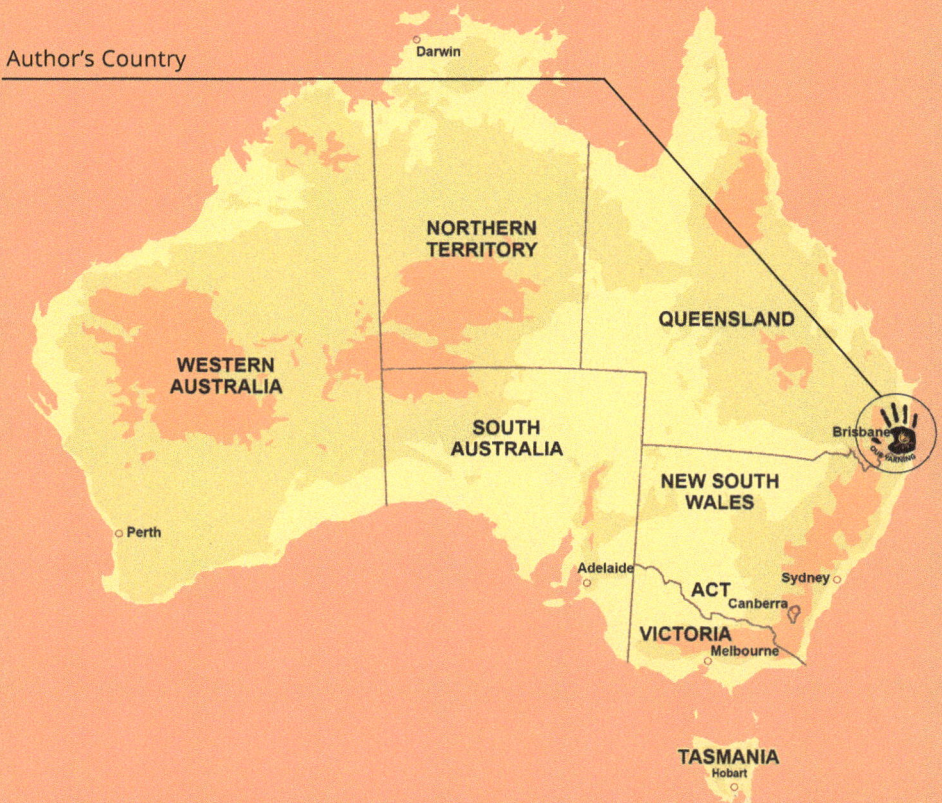

Author's Country

Darwin

NORTHERN
TERRITORY

QUEENSLAND

WESTERN
AUSTRALIA

SOUTH
AUSTRALIA

Brisbane

Perth

NEW SOUTH
WALES

Adelaide

ACT   Sydney
Canberra

VICTORIA
Melbourne

TASMANIA
Hobart

Our Yarning

The Our Yarning collection aligns with the Australian Curriculum through the Cross-Curriculum Priorities — Aboriginal and Torres Strait Islander Histories and Cultures. The collection provides an authentic opportunity for learning and embedding Aboriginal and Torres Strait Islander perspectives because it is written by Aboriginal and Torres Strait Islander people.

We know that children learn better, and enjoy reading more, when they see themselves in the stories, characters and illustrations of the books they read.

To download the app, visit the Google Play Store or Apple Store and search 'Our Yarning'.

libraryforall.org

You're reading Middle Primary

Learner – Beginner readers

Start your reading journey with short words, big ideas and plenty of pictures.

Level 1 – Rising readers

Raise your reading level with more words, simple sentences and exciting images.

Level 2 – Eager readers

Enjoy your reading time with familiar words, but complex sentences.

Level 3 – Progressing readers

Develop your reading skills with creative stories and some challenging vocabulary.

Level 4 – Fluent readers

Step up your reading skills with playful narratives, new words and fun facts.

Middle Primary – Curious readers

Discover your world through science and stories.

Upper Primary – Adventurous readers

Explore your world through science and stories.

Recipes from Community

First published 2025

Published by Library For All Ltd
Email: info@libraryforall.org
URL: libraryforall.org

Our Yarning logo design by Jason Lee, Bidjipidji Art

Original illustrations by Nerida Groom

Recipes from Community
Community of Little Ducks Annerley in collaboration with JBus
ISBN: 978-1-923485-31-0
SKU04657